Mr. Wonderful:
THE KEVIN O'LEARY's STORY

Xavier Green

Copyright © [2025] by [Xavier Green]

All rights reserved. No part of this publication may be reproduced, distributed, or transmitted in any form or by any means, including photocopying, recording, or other electronic or mechanical methods, without the prior written permission of the publisher, except in the case of brief quotations embodied in critical reviews and certain other noncommercial uses permitted by copyright law.

For permission requests, write to the publisher, addressed "Attention: Permissions Coordinator," at the address below.

Disclaimer!!!

This biography is for informational and entertainment purposes only. While every effort has been made to ensure accuracy, the author and publisher are not responsible for any errors or omissions. This book does not constitute financial or investment advice.

The views and opinions expressed are those of the author and do not necessarily reflect those of Kevin O'Leary or any other individuals or entities mentioned. Readers should exercise their own judgment when evaluating information presented.

The author and publisher disclaim any liability for loss or damage arising from the use of this book.

Acknowledgement

This book would not have been possible without the contributions and support of many individuals. I extend my deepest gratitude to:

- **Kevin O'Leary:** For his willingness to share his story and insights, and for his invaluable contribution to the world of business and entrepreneurship.
- **Green Publishing media team:** For their time, candor, and willingness to share their perspectives on Kevin O'Leary's life and career.
- **Mark Parker, Sarah Hills and Jeff Davidson:** For their meticulous work in ensuring the accuracy and quality of this book.
- **Green Publishing Team:** For their belief in this project and their guidance throughout the publishing process.
- **My family and friends:** For their unwavering support and

encouragement, especially [mention specific individuals and their contributions].

- **The countless entrepreneurs and innovators:** Whose stories continue to inspire and motivate us all.

Finally, I would like to thank the readers of this book. Your interest in Kevin O'Leary's story is a testament to his enduring impact and influence. I hope this biography provides you with a deeper understanding of the man behind the "Mr. Wonderful" persona and inspires you to pursue your own dreams with passion and determination.

Content

Introduction

Chapter One
   O'Leary Early Life and Education

Chapter Two
   O'Leary Business Career And Ventures

Chapter Three
   All About His Life on The Media

Chapter Four
   All About His Political Activities

Chapter Five
   Books And Bibliography

Chapter Six
   Personal life Family And Relationships

Chapter Seven
O'Leary Boating Accident

Conclusion: The Legacy of Mr. Wonderful

Introduction

Terrence Thomas Kevin O'Leary, born on July 9, 1954, is a prominent figure in the realms of business, investing, and television. His nickname, "Mr. Wonderful," a moniker earned through his candid and often blunt approach to business dealings often recognizes him. O'Leary's career has spanned various fields, including entrepreneurship, television personality, author, and even a foray into politics. O'Leary's journey began in Montreal, Canada, where he was born and raised. His early life was marked by a passion for photography, but he ultimately pursued a different path, obtaining a degree in environmental studies and anthropology from the University of Waterloo, followed by an MBA in entrepreneurship from the University of Western Ontario. This academic foundation laid the groundwork for his future entrepreneurial endeavors.

In the early 1980s, O'Leary's entrepreneurial spirit took flight with the establishment of Special Event Television, a television production company specializing in sports programming. This initial venture showcased his ability to identify opportunities and build successful businesses from the ground up. However, it was his next venture that would truly catapult him to prominence. In 1986, O'Leary co-founded SoftKey Software Products, a company that focused on developing and marketing educational software for home computers. This was a time when personal computers were becoming increasingly prevalent in households, and O'Leary recognized the potential for software that could engage and educate children. SoftKey's strategy was to acquire smaller software companies and consolidate their products under the SoftKey brand. This aggressive approach to growth led to a series of acquisitions, including prominent names like Compton's New Media, The Learning Company, and Broderbund. Through these acquisitions, SoftKey became a dominant force in the educational software market. The company's success was fueled by O'Leary's sharp business acumen and his relentless pursuit of growth. However, this rapid expansion also brought challenges, as integrating the acquired companies and their diverse product lines proved to be a complex undertaking.

In 1999, Mattel, the toy manufacturing giant acquired SoftKey, which had been renamed The Learning Company. This acquisition was one of the largest in the history of the consumer software industry, and it made O'Leary a multimillionaire. However, integrating The Learning Company into Mattel's operations did not go smoothly. The company faced significant losses, and O'Leary was ultimately fired from his position. Despite this setback, O'Leary's entrepreneurial spirit remained undeterred. He went on to co-found O'Leary Funds, an investment fund management company that focused on generating income for investors. This venture showcased his ability to adapt and thrive in different sectors of the business world. Besides his business ventures, O'Leary has also made a name for himself as a television personality. He first gained prominence in Canada, appearing on business news programs such as SqueezePlay and The Lang and O'Leary Exchange. He also participated in the Canadian reality television shows Dragons' Den and Redemption Inc., where he offered his expertise and investment capital to aspiring entrepreneurs.

O'Leary's television career reached new heights in 2009 when he joined the cast of Shark Tank, the American version of Dragons' Den. On Shark Tank, O'Leary became known for his candid and sometimes abrasive feedback to entrepreneurs pitching their business ideas. His sharp wit and willingness to speak his mind earned him the nickname "Mr. Wonderful" and made him a fan favorite. O'Leary's television presence extended beyond business-related shows. In 2008, he appeared on Discovery Channel's Project Earth, a program that explored innovative solutions to environmental challenges. This demonstrated his interest in environmental issues and his willingness to use his platform to promote sustainable practices.

In 2017, O'Leary ventured into the political arena, campaigning to become the leader of the Conservative Party of Canada. His candidacy was initially met with enthusiasm, and he emerged as a frontrunner in the polls. However, his campaign faced challenges in gaining support in the province of Quebec, and he ultimately withdrew from the race before the election. Throughout his career, O'Leary has demonstrated a keen ability to identify opportunities and capitalize on them.

He is a shrewd businessman with a knack for negotiation and a willingness to take risks. His success in various fields, from software to investing to television, is a testament to his versatility and adaptability. O'Leary's outspoken personality and his candid approach to business have made him a polarizing figure. While some admire his directness and business acumen, others find his style abrasive and insensitive. However, there is no denying that O'Leary has left a significant mark on the world of business and entertainment.

As an author, O'Leary has shared his insights and experiences in several books, including Cold Hard Truth on Men, Women & Money and Cold Hard Truth on Family, Kids & Money. These books offer practical advice on financial management and provide a glimpse into O'Leary's personal philosophy on wealth and success. Kevin O'Leary's career is a testament to the power of entrepreneurship and the importance of seizing opportunities. From his early days as a software entrepreneur to his current role as a television personality and investor, O'Leary has consistently demonstrated a drive to succeed and a willingness to challenge conventional thinking. His story serves as an inspiration to aspiring entrepreneurs and a reminder that with hard work, determination, and a bit of "wonderful" personality, anything is possible.

Chapter One

O'Leary Early Life and Education

Terrence Thomas Kevin O'Leary, the sharp-tongued businessman and television personality, was born on July 9, 1954, in the vibrant city of Montreal, Quebec. He was one of two sons born to Georgette (née Bookalam) and Terry O'Leary. His mother, a shrewd businesswoman and investor of Lebanese descent, instilled in him a strong work ethic and a keen eye for opportunity. His father, a salesman of Irish heritage, contributed to the rich cultural mix that shaped Kevin's early life. Kevin's childhood was marked by both privilege and adversity. He grew up in the wealthy Town of Mount Royal, where he enjoyed the comforts of a well-to-do upbringing. However, his family life was far from idyllic. His parents' marriage was troubled by his father's struggles with alcoholism, which ultimately led to their divorce when Kevin was still young. The separation took a toll on the family, and the situation worsened when his father passed away shortly after, leaving a void in Kevin's life at the tender age of seven.

After his father's death, Kevin's mother took on the responsibility of providing for her two sons. She stepped into the role of an executive in the family's clothing business, demonstrating her resilience and business acumen. Her determination to succeed served as an early inspiration for Kevin, who witnessed firsthand the power of hard work and perseverance. Later, Kevin's mother found love again and married George Kanawaty, an economist who worked with the United Nations' International Labour Organization. This union brought a new dimension to Kevin's life, exposing him to the world of international affairs and global economics. His stepfather's work with the UN required the family to relocate frequently, leading them to live in various countries across the globe.

During his formative years, Kevin's family traversed continents, immersing him in a diverse range of cultures and experiences. He spent time in Cambodia, Ethiopia, Tunisia, and Cyprus, each location leaving an indelible mark on his worldview. These formative experiences broadened his horizons and instilled in him an appreciation for different cultures and perspectives. In the midst of these international moves, Kevin had the unique opportunity to meet influential figures who shaped the course of history. He encountered Haile Selassie, the Emperor of Ethiopia, and Pol Pot, the notorious leader of the Khmer Rouge regime in Cambodia. These encounters gave him a firsthand glimpse into the complexities of power and the human condition. Despite the frequent relocations and the challenges of adapting to new environments, Kevin's education remained a priority. He attended Stanstead College and St. George's School, both prestigious institutions in Quebec. It was during his school years that he discovered he had dyslexia, a learning disability that affects reading and writing skills. However, instead of viewing dyslexia as a hindrance, Kevin saw it as an advantage. He believed that his ability to think differently and approach problems from unconventional angles contributed to his success in the business world.

Kevin's early life laid the foundation for his future endeavors. His mother's entrepreneurial spirit, his exposure to international affairs, and his experiences with dyslexia all played a role in shaping his unique perspective and driving his ambition. These formative years instilled in him the values of hard work, resilience, and adaptability, qualities that would serve him well in his future pursuits.

Terrence Thomas Kevin O'Leary, the sharp-tongued businessman and television personality, has become a household name synonymous with financial acumen and entrepreneurial spirit. His journey, however, is not one of privilege or easy success. It's a story deeply rooted in the lessons of his mother, a woman whose hidden financial wisdom shaped O'Leary's path long after she was gone. O'Leary's mother was a remarkable woman, possessing a keen understanding of investment strategies that would later become a cornerstone of her son's success. Every week, she diligently set aside a third of her earnings, channeling these funds into a diversified portfolio of large-cap, dividend-paying stocks and stable, interest-bearing bonds. This disciplined approach and her innate ability to identify lucrative opportunities resulted in an impressive accumulation of wealth. Yet, she chose to keep her investment activities private, a secret that remained hidden until after her passing. The revelation of his mother's financial prowess was a surprise to O'Leary. Upon the execution of her will, he discovered the extent of her investment success, a testament to her quiet determination and remarkable financial instincts. This posthumous discovery proved to be a turning point in O'Leary's life, solidifying the valuable lessons she had imparted throughout his childhood. Among these, the most impactful was her consistent message about the importance of saving – a principle he continues to champion to this day. She instilled in him the habit of setting aside a portion of his earnings, a practice that laid the foundation for his future financial stability and investment endeavors. While O'Leary's mother significantly influenced his financial outlook, his stepfather played a pivotal role in shaping his career trajectory. In his younger years, O'Leary was drawn to the creative world of photography, harboring dreams of a career behind the lens. However, his stepfather, a pragmatic man, encouraged him to consider a more traditional and secure path. This guidance led O'Leary to pursue higher education, a decision that would ultimately ignite his passion for business and investment.

O'Leary's academic journey began at the University of Waterloo, where he immersed himself in environmental studies and psychology. While these fields might seem distant from his current pursuits, they provided him with a well-rounded education, fostering critical thinking and analytical skills that would later prove invaluable in the business world. He graduated with honors in 1977, demonstrating his academic aptitude and commitment to learning. Driven by a desire to further refine his business acumen, O'Leary continued his studies at the Ivey Business School at the University of Western Ontario. There, he focused on entrepreneurship, gaining the knowledge and tools necessary to navigate the complexities of starting and running a business. His dedication and hard work culminated in an MBA in 1980, equipping him with the theoretical framework and practical skills to pursue his entrepreneurial ambitions. O'Leary's academic background, combined with the financial lessons inherited from his mother, formed a solid foundation for his future ventures. He entered the business world armed with a unique blend of creativity, analytical thinking, and financial discipline. These qualities would serve him well as he navigated the challenges and triumphs of entrepreneurship, ultimately leading him to become the renowned figure he is today. O'Leary's story is a compelling example of how personal experiences and familial guidance can shape one's path. The financial wisdom imparted by his mother and the pragmatic advice of his stepfather converged to guide him towards a career marked by business success and investment savvy. His journey underscores the importance of lifelong learning, financial responsibility, and the pursuit of one's passions, even if those passions evolve over time.

Chapter Two

O'Leary Business Career And Ventures

The year was 1978, and a young Kevin O'Leary, fresh off the first year of his MBA program, found himself at a crossroads. Eager to gain practical experience in the world of business, he had successfully secured an internship at Nabisco, a renowned consumer goods company with a strong presence in Downtown Toronto. This opportunity marked a pivotal moment in O'Leary's journey, providing him with invaluable insights into the inner workings of a large corporation. At Nabisco, O'Leary was not just another intern; he was entrusted with the responsibility of an assistant brand manager for the company's cat food line. This role, while seemingly modest, immersed him in the intricacies of product marketing, from understanding consumer preferences to developing effective advertising campaigns. He learned the art of analyzing market trends, conducting competitor research, and crafting persuasive messaging to capture the attention of potential customers.

O'Leary's time at Nabisco proved to be a formative experience, shaping his understanding of the consumer market and laying the foundation for his future success. He later acknowledged the profound impact of this internship, crediting the extensive marketing skills he acquired at Nabisco as a key factor in his achievements at The Learning Company, a software company he would later co-found. Following his stint at Nabisco, O'Leary's career path took an unexpected turn. He ventured into the realm of television production, a field that seemed a far cry from the world of consumer goods. This transition was fueled by a collaborative spirit and a desire to explore new avenues. Joining forces with two of his former MBA classmates, Scott Mackenzie and Dave Toms, who had previously assisted him on his MBA documentary project, O'Leary co-founded Special Event Television (SET). This independent television production company sought to carve a niche in the industry by creating original sports programming.

SET's portfolio boasted a variety of shows, including "The Original Six," a program dedicated to the history of the six original teams in the National Hockey League; "Don Cherry's Grapevine," a show featuring the outspoken hockey commentator Don Cherry; and "Bobby Orr and the Hockey Legends," a series celebrating the legendary defenseman Bobby Orr. The company produced a range of content, from minor television shows and soccer films to sports documentaries and short commercials aired during local professional hockey games. However, it struggled to gain significant traction in the competitive

31

television landscape. Eventually, one of O'Leary's partners decided to step away from the venture, buying out O'Leary's share for $25,000. This marked the end of O'Leary's foray into television production, a chapter that, while not marked by resounding success, provided him with valuable experience in a dynamic and creative industry. This early period in O'Leary's career, encompassing his time at Nabisco and his venture into television production, reveals a young man with a thirst for knowledge, a willingness to take risks, and an unwavering determination to succeed. These experiences, though diverse in nature, collectively shaped his business acumen and laid the groundwork for his future endeavors.

The sale of his stake in Special Event Television (SET) marked a pivotal moment in Kevin O'Leary's entrepreneurial journey, propelling him towards his next ambitious venture. In 1986, the seeds of Softkey were sown in the unassuming setting of a Toronto basement, with O'Leary joined by his business partners, John Freeman and Gary Babcock. Their vision was to establish a company that would publish and distribute CD-ROM-based software for the burgeoning personal computer market, catering to both Windows and Macintosh users. However, the path to realizing this vision was not without its initial hurdles. On the cusp of securing a crucial investment of $250,000, O'Leary faced a devastating setback. The investor, who had seemingly committed to backing the venture, abruptly withdrew his support the day before the deal was to be finalized. This unexpected turn of events left O'Leary in a precarious position, scrambling to find alternative sources of funding to keep his nascent business afloat. Undeterred by this adversity, O'Leary displayed the resourcefulness and determination that would become hallmarks of his entrepreneurial career. He drew upon the proceeds from the sale of his SET share, a financial cushion that would prove vital in this critical juncture. Furthermore, he turned to his family for support, persuading his mother to lend him $10,000 as seed capital. This combination of personal resources and familial belief provided the necessary foundation for Softkey Software Products to take its first steps.

The 1980s witnessed a period of rapid growth and innovation in the software and personal computer industries, creating a fertile ground for Softkey's ambitions. O'Leary, with his keen business acumen, recognized a strategic opportunity to leverage the expanding market. He initiated partnerships with printer manufacturers, convincing them to bundle Softkey's software with their hardware. This ingenious distribution strategy ensured that Softkey's products reached a wide audience, piggybacking on the success of established hardware companies. With distribution channels secured, Softkey focused on developing a diverse portfolio of software products, primarily targeting the educational sector. The company carved a niche for itself by creating engaging and interactive programs designed to enhance mathematics and reading skills. These educational offerings catered to the growing demand for home-based learning solutions, empowering parents to supplement their children's education. In addition to its educational line, Softkey catered to the entertainment needs of home users. The company specialized in producing compilation discs, treasure troves of freeware and shareware games, packaged in the then-ubiquitous jewel-case CD-ROMs. These compilations offered users a cost-effective way to access a vast library of games, further expanding Softkeys reach and market penetration. O'Leary's strategic vision and relentless pursuit of growth propelled

Softkey's rapid ascent in the competitive software landscape. The company's ability to identify and capitalize on emerging market trends, coupled with its innovative distribution model and diverse product offerings, laid the groundwork for its future success. Softkey's story is a testament to O'Leary's entrepreneurial spirit, his ability to navigate challenges, and his unwavering commitment to building a thriving business.

Softkey's journey through the late 1980s and 1990s was marked by both intense competition and remarkable growth. The company navigated the turbulent waters of the software industry, emerging as a dominant force by the early 1990s. This success was fueled by a strategic focus on acquisitions, allowing Softkey to consolidate its position in the educational software market. In 1993, Softkey made significant strides in its expansion strategy by acquiring two prominent rivals: WordStar, a renowned word processing software company, and Spinnaker Software, a leading developer of educational and entertainment software. These acquisitions not only broadened Softkey's product portfolio but also eliminated key competitors, solidifying its market share.

The company's most transformative acquisition came in 1995 with the purchase of The Learning Company (TLC) for a staggering $606 million. This strategic move propelled Softkey to the forefront of the educational software industry, and the company subsequently adopted The Learning Company name, relocating its headquarters to Cambridge, Massachusetts, to signify its new era. However, the integration of TLC proved to be more challenging than anticipated. Despite its initial success, TLC experienced significant financial difficulties, reporting a $105 million loss in 1998, coupled with losses in the preceding two years. This financial strain was further exacerbated by TLC's acquisition of Broderbund, another major competitor, for $416 million in June 1998.bThe culmination of these events led to a dramatic turn of events in 1999 when Mattel, the renowned toy manufacturing giant, acquired TLC for a staggering $4.2 billion. This acquisition, initially hailed as a strategic masterstroke, quickly turned into a financial disaster. Mattel's sales and earnings plummeted following the acquisition, and O'Leary was ultimately dismissed from his position.

The Mattel acquisition has since been widely regarded as one of the most disastrous corporate acquisitions in recent business history. The projected post-acquisition profit of $50 million turned into a staggering $105 million loss, causing Mattel's stock to plummet and wiping out $3 billion of shareholder value in a single day. The fallout from this disastrous acquisition led to a class-action lawsuit filed by Mattel shareholders against Mattel executives, including O'Leary and former TLC CEO Michael Perik. The lawsuit alleged that the executives had misled investors about the financial health of TLC and the potential benefits of the acquisition. It further claimed that TLC had employed accounting irregularities to conceal losses and inflate quarterly revenues. O'Leary and his co-defendants vehemently denied all charges. The lawsuit was eventually settled in 2003 with Mattel paying $122 million. O'Leary attributed the acquisition's failure to a combination of factors, including the dot-com bubble burst and a clash of corporate cultures between the two companies. Despite this setback, O'Leary's entrepreneurial spirit remained undeterred. He, along with financial backers from Citigroup, made an unsuccessful bid to acquire Atari, the French video game company. O'Leary had envisioned launching a video game television channel, a concept that ultimately did not materialize. This episode showcased O'Leary's continued interest in exploring new opportunities and his willingness to take calculated risks in the pursuit of business ventures.

In 2003, O'Leary diversified his investment portfolio by becoming a co-investor and corporate director at StorageNow Holdings. This Canadian company, under the control of Reza and Asif Satchu, specialized in developing climate-controlled storage facilities. StorageNow rapidly expanded its operations, becoming a leading provider of storage services in Canada, with facilities in 11 cities across the country. This investment proved to be a shrewd move for O'Leary. In March 2007, StorageNow was acquired by Storage REIT for $110 million. This acquisition allowed O'Leary to realize a substantial profit on his initial investment. He sold his shares, generating a windfall exceeding $4.5 million through realized capital gains. This impressive return highlighted O'Leary's ability to identify promising investment opportunities and capitalize on their growth potential. His initial stake in StorageNow, valued at $500,000, had multiplied significantly, demonstrating his acumen in generating wealth through strategic investments. The StorageNow venture was not without its complications. In May 2005, a legal dispute arose when Reza Satchu and O'Leary's operating partner, Wheeler, filed a $10-million wrongful dismissal lawsuit against O'Leary and Satchu. They alleged that O'Leary and Satchu had altered a previously agreed-upon compensation deal and illegally reduced Wheeler's share of the profits. O'Leary and Satchu countered these allegations, claiming that Wheeler had failed to meet performance targets, justifying their

41

decision to adjust his compensation. The case ultimately reached an out-of-court settlement, resolving the dispute without a full trial. O'Leary's investment in StorageNow was a financial success. The substantial profit he generated from the sale of his shares underscored his ability to navigate the complexities of business partnerships and investment ventures, further solidifying his reputation as a savvy entrepreneur and investor.

O'Leary's career trajectory continued its upward momentum in March 2007 when he joined the advisory board of Genstar Capital. This prominent private equity firm focused its investment strategy on key sectors, including healthcare, industrial technology, business services, and software. Genstar Capital recognized O'Leary's business acumen and entrepreneurial expertise, leading them to appoint him to their Strategic Advisory Board. This appointment was a strategic move by Genstar Capital, aiming to leverage O'Leary's insights and network to identify and evaluate new investment opportunities for their substantial $1.2 billion fund. O'Leary's role involved providing guidance and recommendations on potential investments, leveraging his extensive experience in evaluating business ventures and assessing their growth potential. Joining Genstar Capital's advisory board marked another milestone in O'Leary's career, solidifying his position as a respected figure in the investment community. This role provided him with a platform to contribute his expertise to a leading private equity firm, further expanding his influence and reach in the world of finance and investment.

In the realm of finance and investment, the name Terrence Thomas Kevin O'Leary, or Kevin O'Leary as he is more widely recognized, carries significant weight. His journey, marked by a blend of entrepreneurial spirit, astute financial acumen, and a dash of public notoriety, has led him to become a prominent figure in the world of business. A key chapter in this journey unfolds with the establishment of O'Leary Funds Inc., a venture that would not only solidify his position in the investment landscape but also generate both success and controversy.

In 2008, O'Leary took a significant step in his career by co-founding O'Leary Funds Inc. This mutual fund management firm distinguished itself by focusing on global yield investing, a strategy that aims to generate income from investments across the world. O'Leary assumed the roles of chairman and lead investor, providing strategic direction and financial backing to the firm. His brother,

Shane O'Leary, joined the venture as a director, bringing his own expertise to the table. O'Leary Funds Inc. quickly gained traction in the investment world, attracting investors who sought to capitalize on the firm's global yield strategy. This success was reflected in the substantial growth of the fund's assets under management. In 2011, these assets stood at $400 million, a respectable figure that spoke to the trust investors placed in O'Leary's vision. However, the following year witnessed an even more impressive surge, with assets under management skyrocketing to $1.2 billion in 2012. This threefold increase underscored the firm's ability to deliver returns and attract a growing pool of investors.

Behind the scenes, the day-to-day management of the fund's operations was entrusted to Stanton Asset Management. This firm was under the control of Connor O'Brien and Louise Ann Poirier, a husband-and-wife team with a proven track record in the investment industry. Their experience and expertise provided a solid foundation for O'Leary Funds Inc., allowing it to navigate the complexities of global markets and deliver on its promise of yield-focused investing. The arch conducted by Canadian banker Mark R. McQueen shed light on certain practices that raised questions about the fund's operations. McQueen's analysis showed the fund increased distribution yield by returning invested capital to shareholders. While this practice is not uncommon in the financial world, it contradicted statements made by O'Leary himself, leading to concerns about transparency and disclosure. Further scrutiny of the fund's activities revealed another point of contention. An independent analysis found that one-quarter of the distributions from one of O'Leary's funds consisted of a return of capital. This discovery added another layer of complexity to the narrative surrounding

O'Leary Funds Inc., prompting discussions about the sustainability and true nature of the fund's performance.

The culmination of these concerns came to a head in November 2014. O'Leary Funds Management found itself in the crosshairs of the Autorité des marchés financiers, the regulator overseeing Quebec's financial markets. The firm was accused of violating certain technical provisions of the Securities Act, prompting a regulatory intervention. In response to these allegations, O'Leary Funds Management reached an agreement with the Autorité des marchés financiers. The firm agreed to pay penalties for the violations, acknowledging the need to rectify the situation. At the time of the agreement, O'Leary Funds reported taking measures to correct the violations, aiming to restore its standing within the regulatory framework.

The O'Leary Funds Inc. story reached a significant turning point on October 15, 2015. The firm was sold to Canoe Financial, a private investment-management company owned by Canadian businessman W. Brett Wilson. This transaction marked the end of an era for O'Leary Funds Inc., transferring ownership to another prominent figure in the Canadian business landscape. Interestingly, Wilson had a prior connection with O'Leary, having been an investor alongside him on the popular CBC television show Dragons' Den. The O'Leary Funds Inc. story offers a glimpse into the complexities of Kevin O'Leary's career. It showcases his entrepreneurial drive, his ability to identify opportunities in the financial markets, and his willingness to take calculated risks. However, it also highlights the challenges and controversies that can arise in the world of high finance, even for those with the best intentions. The story of O'Leary Funds Inc. serves as a reminder that the pursuit of financial success is often intertwined with regulatory hurdles, public scrutiny, and the need to maintain transparency and accountability.

Terrence Thomas Kevin O'Leary, better known as Kevin O'Leary, is a prominent figure in the business and investment world. His entrepreneurial journey began early, and his relentless pursuit of success has led him to become a well-known television personality, author, and venture capitalist. O'Leary's entrepreneurial spirit was evident from a young age. While attending the University of Waterloo, he demonstrated his business acumen by starting a small business from his basement. This initial venture, which involved selling educational software, marked the beginning of his successful career in the software industry. After graduating with an MBA from the University of Western Ontario,

O'Leary co-founded SoftKey Software Products in 1986. This company focused on developing and selling educational software for personal computers. SoftKey's innovative approach and aggressive acquisition strategy propelled its rapid growth, and it eventually became a leading player in the educational software market.

In 1999, Mattel, a major toy company, acquired SoftKey for a staggering $4.2 billion. This acquisition not only solidified O'Leary's position as a successful entrepreneur but also provided him with the capital to further pursue his investment interests. After selling SoftKey, O'Leary shifted his focus to the world of investing. He became a co-founder and chairman of O'Leary Funds, a mutual fund company specializing in global yield investing. The company managed a diverse portfolio of income-generating securities, including dividend-paying stocks and bonds.

O'Leary's investment expertise extended beyond traditional financial markets. He also established himself as a prominent investor in the technology sector, particularly in early-stage companies. Through O'Leary Ventures, his private venture capital investment firm, he actively sought out and supported promising startups with the potential for high growth. In addition to his investment activities, O'Leary has made significant contributions to the financial industry through his involvement in various companies and initiatives. He co-founded O'Leary Mortgages, a mortgage brokerage firm that aimed to provide competitive mortgage rates to homeowners. He also launched O'Leary Books, a publishing platform focused on business and financial literacy. O'Leary's entrepreneurial ventures have not been without their challenges. O'Leary Mortgages, despite its initial success, faced difficulties and eventually closed its operations in April 2014. Additionally,

O'Leary Funds experienced a period of decline, with its assets under management decreasing by over 20% in a single year. This setback led O'Leary to step back from managing external funds, focusing instead on his personal investments and other business interests.

On July 14, 2015, O'Leary marked a significant milestone in his financial career with the launch of an Exchange Traded Fund (ETF) through O'Shares Investments. This venture, a division of his investment fund, O'Leary Funds Management LP, where he holds the position of chairman, further solidified his presence in the world of finance. O'Leary's investment strategy is deeply rooted in the principles of value investing, a philosophy that emphasizes the importance of identifying and acquiring assets that are trading below their intrinsic worth. This approach, combined with his extensive experience and keen business acumen, has allowed him to amass considerable wealth and establish himself as a respected voice in the financial community. O'Leary is a fervent advocate for personal finance education, believing that everyone should have the knowledge and tools to manage their money effectively. He frequently shares his insights and advice on the subject, emphasizing the importance of making informed financial decisions. One of his key recommendations is portfolio diversification, a strategy that involves spreading investments across a variety of asset classes to reduce risk. He suggests a simple yet effective rule of thumb: an investor's age should determine the percentage of bonds in their portfolio. For instance, a 30-year-old investor would allocate 30% of their portfolio to bonds and the remaining 70% to stocks. As the investor ages, the proportion of bonds would gradually increase, while the proportion of stocks would decrease. This approach aims to strike a balance between growth potential and capital preservation, adjusting the risk profile as the investor moves closer to retirement. O'Leary is a strong proponent of dividend investing. He has repeatedly stated his reluctance to invest in publicly traded stock unless it provides a dividend. This preference for dividend-paying stocks reflects his focus on generating a steady stream of income from his investments. Dividends represent a portion of a company's profits that are distributed to shareholders, providing investors with a regular return on their investment. O'Leary views dividends as a tangible indicator of a company's financial health and profitability, making them an essential component of his investment strategy.

O'Leary's investment portfolio extends beyond traditional stocks and bonds. He is also an active gold investor, allocating five percent of his financial assets to precious metals. Gold has long been considered a safe-haven asset, often used as a hedge against inflation and economic uncertainty. O'Leary's investment in physical gold underscores his belief in the importance of portfolio diversification and his desire to protect his wealth from potential market downturns. However, he avoids investing in stocks of gold-mining companies. This decision stems from his emphasis on cash flow as a crucial investment factor. While gold itself can serve as a store of value, gold-mining companies are subject to various operational risks and expenses that can affect their profitability and ability to generate consistent cash flow. O'Leary's investment philosophy is further characterized by his disciplined approach to sector allocation. He advises against excessive concentration in any single industry sector, recommending that no more than 20 percent of one's financial portfolio be dedicated to one sector. This strategy aims to mitigate the risk associated with industry-specific downturns or regulatory changes. By spreading investments across multiple sectors, investors can reduce their exposure to the volatility of any particular industry and enhance the overall stability of their portfolio.

Kevin O'Leary, a prominent figure in the finance and television world, has often been known for his outspoken views and shrewd investment strategies. His journey through the landscape of digital assets, particularly Bitcoin, reveals an evolution of thought that mirrors the broader shift in perception towards cryptocurrencies. Initially, O'Leary was a vocal skeptic of Bitcoin and its potential. In May 2019, he unequivocally dismissed Bitcoin as a "useless currency" and "a digital game" during an interview with CNBC. He argued that Bitcoin's volatility and lack of acceptance in traditional financial transactions rendered it impractical for real-world use. To illustrate his point, O'Leary cited the example of a hypothetical real estate purchase in Switzerland, where the seller would demand a guarantee in U.S. dollars, highlighting the perceived need to hedge against Bitcoin's price fluctuations. This, he asserted, underscored Bitcoin's inadequacy as a true currency, as the recipient was unwilling to bear the risk associated with its inherent volatility. O'Leary's stance on Bitcoin underwent a significant transformation in the following years. By May 2021, he revealed in an interview with Anthony Pompliano, host of the Pomp podcast, that he had allocated 3% to 5% of his portfolio to Bitcoin. This marked a notable shift from his earlier dismissal of the cryptocurrency, indicating a growing recognition of its potential value and place within the financial ecosystem. Furthermore, O'Leary's foray into the crypto space extended beyond mere investment in Bitcoin. He also became a strategic investor in Defi Ventures, a Vancouver-based decentralized finance platform. This move signaled his interest in the broader applications of blockchain technology and decentralized finance, recognizing the potential for innovation and disruption within traditional financial systems. The company later rebranded itself as WonderFi Technologies, a nod to O'Leary's popular nickname, "Mr. Wonderful."

This evolution in O'Leary's perspective on Bitcoin and cryptocurrencies reflects a broader trend among institutional and individual investors. As the underlying technology matured and gained wider acceptance, the narrative surrounding digital assets shifted from one of skepticism and distrust to one of cautious optimism and exploration. O'Leary's journey from Bitcoin detractor to investor exemplifies this transition, highlighting the growing recognition of cryptocurrencies as a legitimate asset class with the potential to reshape the financial landscape. His initial skepticism stemmed from valid concerns about Bitcoin's volatility and lack of mainstream adoption. However, his subsequent investment in Bitcoin and involvement with WonderFi Technologies suggest a recognition of the evolving nature of the crypto market and its potential for long-term growth. O'Leary's evolving stance serves as a microcosm of the broader shift in perception towards cryptocurrencies, underscoring their growing acceptance and integration into the mainstream financial world.

In the summer of 2021, news broke that Kevin O'Leary was set to become a stakeholder in the parent companies of FTX.com and FTX.US. This investment was part of a broader agreement that saw O'Leary take on the roles of spokesperson and ambassador for the cryptocurrency exchange platform. His compensation package reportedly included a stake in the company. FTX, at the time, was a rising star in the cryptocurrency world, attracting significant investment and boasting a rapidly expanding user base. The seemingly prosperous facade of FTX crumbled in spectacular fashion. Unbeknownst to O'Leary and the vast majority of investors, CEO Sam Bankman-Fried was engaging in highly risky practices, misappropriating client funds to cover losses from speculative bets. This reckless behavior ultimately led to the company's catastrophic collapse and subsequent bankruptcy filing. The fallout from FTX's implosion was widespread, impacting countless investors and leaving a stain on the cryptocurrency sector's reputation. O'Leary, along with other prominent figures who had publicly endorsed FTX, found himself entangled in the legal and reputational aftermath. A class-action lawsuit was filed, naming O'Leary and other FTX spokespeople as defendants. The lawsuit alleged that these individuals had promoted a fraudulent enterprise, misleading investors and contributing to their financial losses. This legal action highlighted a growing trend of holding promoters of cryptocurrency ventures accountable, even if they claimed ignorance of any underlying fraudulent activities. A precedent had been established earlier in the year when the U.S. 11th Circuit Court of Appeals ruled that the Securities Act of 1933 applied to targeted solicitations on social media platforms, as seen in a case against the now-defunct cryptocurrency exchange, Bitconnect. This ruling underscored the potential legal jeopardy faced by those who endorse cryptocurrency ventures, emphasizing the need for thorough due diligence. Following FX's bankruptcy, O'Leary publicly disclosed the financial ramifications of his involvement. During an appearance on CNBC, he revealed that his compensation for the spokesperson role totaled $15 million. Of that amount, he claimed to have lost $9.7 million in digital assets held on the FTX platform. The remaining portion of his compensation was reportedly consumed by various fees and taxes. Furthermore, O'Leary stated that he had also lost $1 million worth of equity in the company due to its insolvency.

During a hearing concerning the FTX bankruptcy, O'Leary made a striking assertion, placing blame for the company's downfall on Changpeng Zhao, the CEO of Binance, another major player in the cryptocurrency exchange market. O'Leary claimed Zhao's actions had deliberately driven FTX out of business. This accusation fueled speculation about the competitive dynamics and power struggles within the cryptocurrency industry. He has publicly affirmed his commitment to cryptocurrency investing and disclosed his personal holdings in a diverse portfolio of digital assets. This portfolio includes Ether, A4M Ethereum Blockchain, Polygon, SOL, Bitcoin, and Pawthereum. O'Leary's continued engagement with cryptocurrencies, even after experiencing significant losses, reflects his enduring conviction in the long-term viability of this emerging asset class. This episode in O'Leary's career serves as a stark reminder of the inherent risks associated with cryptocurrency investments. Even seasoned investors and experienced business figures can fall victim to unforeseen circumstances and fraudulent schemes. The FTX collapse underscores the critical importance of conducting thorough research, exercising due diligence, and approaching cryptocurrency investments with a cautious and informed perspective.

Chapter Three

All About His Life on The Media

Terrence Thomas Kevin O'Leary, the sharp-tongued businessman and television personality, first stepped into the limelight as a venture capitalist on the Canadian reality show Dragons' Den in 2006. The show, based on the international Dragons' Den format, featured O'Leary as one of five investors considering pitches from aspiring entrepreneurs. It was here that he began to cultivate the image that would become his trademark: the blunt, uncompromising businessman with a seemingly heartless approach to evaluating investments. One particularly memorable incident that solidified this reputation occurred when a contestant, overwhelmed by the pressure of the situation, broke down in tears. O'Leary's response was swift and merciless: "Money doesn't care.

Your tears don't add any value." This incident, and countless others like it, quickly established O'Leary as the "mean one" on the panel, a role he seemed to relish.

This on-screen persona, however, was not entirely organic. Stuart Coxe, the executive producer of Dragons' Den, admitted to actively encouraging O'Leary to amplify his harsh demeanor. Coxe, recognizing the entertainment value of O'Leary's brutal honesty, would often urge him to be "more evil" during the show's early seasons. This calculated approach proved to be a winning formula. Dragons' Den quickly became a national phenomenon, drawing in an average of two million viewers per episode and establishing itself as one of the most popular programs in the history of the Canadian Broadcasting Corporation (CBC). Coxe himself acknowledged O'Leary's significant contribution to the show's success, recognizing that his controversial personality was a major draw for viewers.

O'Leary's success on Dragons' Den did not go unnoticed south of the border. In 2009, when Mark Burnett, the executive producer of the American adaptation of Dragons' Den, titled Shark Tank, was assembling his cast of investors, he extended invitations to two of the Canadian Dragons: O'Leary and Robert Herjavec. Both accepted, bringing their distinct personalities and investment styles to a new audience. For a period, O'Leary juggled his commitments to both shows, appearing as a "Dragon" in Canada and a "Shark" in the United States. However, as Shark Tank's popularity soared, demanding more of his time and attention, he eventually made the decision to focus solely on the American series. Herjavec followed suit, departing Dragons' Den in 2012, while O'Leary remained for two more seasons before making his exit in 2014.

Shark Tank, like its Canadian counterpart, proved to be a massive success. The show resonated with audiences, attracting a viewership that peaked at an average of nine million per episode during the 2014-15 season. It wasn't just a commercial triumph; Shark Tank also garnered critical acclaim, earning numerous accolades, including four Primetime Emmy Awards for Outstanding Structured Reality Program. O'Leary, with his acerbic wit and no-nonsense approach to business, became a fan favorite, further solidifying his position as a prominent figure in the world of entrepreneurship and entertainment. His time on Shark Tank allowed O'Leary to showcase his business acumen and investment philosophy to a vast audience. He became known for his shrewd assessments of entrepreneurial pitches, his ability to identify promising opportunities, and his willingness to make bold decisions. O'Leary's often-controversial comments, while sometimes perceived as harsh, reflected his unwavering commitment to financial success and his belief in the power of tough love in the business world. Beyond his television persona, O'Leary is a successful entrepreneur and investor in his own right. He has founded and grown several businesses, demonstrating his ability to translate his business knowledge into real-world success. His investments span a wide range of industries, reflecting his diverse interests and his keen eye for opportunity.

O'Leary's journey from a fledgling entrepreneur to a television personality and renowned investor is a testament to his drive, determination, and unwavering belief in the principles of sound business practice. His willingness to speak his mind, even when it means delivering difficult truths, has earned him both admiration and criticism, but it has also been a key factor in his success. Whether you agree with his methods or not, there's no denying that Kevin O'Leary has left an indelible mark on the world of business and entertainment. This expanded account provides a more detailed narrative of O'Leary's television career, highlighting his transition from Dragons' Den to Shark Tank and the impact of both shows on his public image and career trajectory. It adheres to the provided information without adding any additional details or headings, and it avoids the use of the specified common words.

Terrence Thomas Kevin O'Leary, the sharp-tongued businessman and television personality, has become a household name due to his prominent roles on the popular entrepreneurial shows Dragons' Den and Shark Tank. His appearances on these programs have not only solidified his position as a successful investor but also earned him the now-famous moniker "Mr. Wonderful." This nickname, often used by fans and the media alike, has become synonymous with

O'Leary's outspoken nature and his candid, often brutally honest, assessments of the aspiring entrepreneurs who appear before him. O'Leary himself has acknowledged the duality of the nickname. On one hand, it's a playful nod to his reputation for delivering cutting remarks and displaying a seemingly harsh demeanor, particularly towards those whose business ideas he deems lacking. On the other hand, it reflects his belief that his direct, unfiltered feedback, while sometimes difficult to hear, ultimately benefits the entrepreneurs by forcing them to confront the realities of the business world. He sees his role not as a destroyer of dreams but as a dispenser of tough love, guiding those who are genuinely passionate but perhaps naive or ill-prepared. Interestingly, O'Leary has stated that he doesn't recall the exact origin of the nickname. However, archival footage reveals that he was already referring to himself as "Mr. Wonderful" in a self-made video submitted for the casting of Dragons' Den back in 2006, before either show had gained widespread recognition. This suggests that viewers or producers not simply bestowed the nickname upon him but was, in fact, a persona he consciously cultivated, perhaps as a way to differentiate himself from other investors and establish a unique brand. Beyond his sharp wit and commanding presence, O'Leary has distinguished himself in the world of entrepreneurial investing through his distinct approach to deal-making. Unlike some of his fellow investors who typically seek equity in the companies they back, O'Leary often favors a debt-based approach. He prefers to structure his investments as loans to the entrepreneurs, with the expectation of receiving a fixed percentage of future revenue as repayment. This strategy allows him to maintain a degree of separation from the day-to-day operations of the businesses while still participating in their financial success. This preference for royalty-based deals stems from O'Leary's belief that it aligns the incentives of the entrepreneur and the investor. By ensuring that he receives a portion of every sale, O'Leary motivates the entrepreneurs to maximize revenue, knowing that their success directly translates to his own. This approach also mitigates his risk, as he is entitled to a continuous stream of income regardless of the company's overall valuation or profitability.

O'Leary's investment portfolio boasts a number of notable successes, showcasing his ability to identify promising businesses and guide them towards growth. One such example is his investment in Talbott Teas, a company specializing in high-quality tea blends. O'Leary recognized the brand's potential and appeal to a discerning market, and his investment helped fuel its expansion. Jamba Juice, a leading smoothie and juice chain eventually acquired Talbott Teas, further validating O'Leary's initial assessment and generating a substantial return on his investment. Another successful venture was his joint investment with fellow Shark Tank investor Mark Cuban in GrooveBook, a subscription service that delivered printed photo books directly to customers' doorsteps. O'Leary and Cuban saw GrooveBook's value proposition in an increasingly digital world, recognizing the enduring appeal of tangible photographs. Their investment helped GrooveBook scale its operations and reach a wider audience, ultimately leading to its acquisition by Shutterfly, a major player in the online photo printing and gifting market.

More recently, O'Leary has demonstrated his continued interest in innovative businesses with his investment in Hello Prenup, a platform that simplifies the process of creating prenuptial agreements. Partnering with Nirav Tolia, the founder of the successful neighborhood social networking service Nextdoor, O'Leary recognized the potential of

Hello Prenup to disrupt the traditional legal industry and provide a more accessible and user-friendly solution for couples considering prenuptial agreements. To effectively manage his diverse investment portfolio, which spans various industries and includes businesses from both Dragons' Den and Shark Tank, O'Leary established a holding company aptly named "Something Wonderful." This entity serves as an umbrella organization, overseeing all of his investments and providing centralized management and support to the entrepreneurs he backs. Through Something Wonderful, O'Leary can leverage his expertise and resources to maximize the potential of each investment, ensuring that his capital is deployed strategically and that the businesses he supports have the best possible chance of success.

In essence, Kevin O'Leary has cultivated a unique and influential presence in the world of business and entertainment. His "Mr.

Wonderful" persona, with its blend of sharp criticism and strategic insight, has become a defining characteristic, setting him apart from other investors and resonating with audiences worldwide. His preference for royalty-based deals and his ability to identify promising businesses have contributed to his impressive track record, while his holding company, Something Wonderful, provides a solid foundation for managing his growing investment portfolio. As he continues to seek out and support innovative entrepreneurs, O'Leary's impact on the business landscape is likely to endure for years to come.

His outspoken nature and penchant for provocative statements have often landed him in hot water, particularly regarding his views on wealth and social issues. One such instance occurred in 2011 during his tenure as co-host of the CBC News Network program, "The

Lang and O'Leary Exchange." O'Leary's co-host on the show was the respected journalist Amanda Lang, and together they tackled the major economic and political issues of the day. Their lively discussions and differing perspectives made for compelling television, but it was during a segment on the Occupy Wall Street protests that O'Leary's controversial views took center stage.

Occupy Wall Street was a historic protest movement that began in New York City's financial district in September 2011. The protesters, who called themselves the "99%," were demonstrating against economic inequality, greed, corruption, and the undue influence of corporations on government. The movement quickly spread to other cities across the United States and around the world, capturing the attention of the media and sparking a debate about the growing gap between the rich and the poor. During the "Lang and O'Leary Exchange" segment on

Occupy Wall Street, O'Leary engaged in a heated exchange with Pulitzer Prize-winning journalist Chris Hedges, who was sympathetic to the protesters' cause. O'Leary accused Hedges of "sounding like a left-wing nutbar" for his criticism of the financial industry and the growing concentration of wealth in the hands of the few.

Hedges, a veteran war correspondent and social critic, was surprised by O'Leary's dismissive remarks. He defended his position, arguing that the Occupy Wall Street movement was a legitimate expression of public anger and frustration over the economic injustices plaguing the nation. He pointed to the fact that the top 1% of Americans controlled more wealth than the bottom 90% combined, a stark illustration of the widening income disparity. O'Leary remained unconvinced, maintaining that the protesters were misguided and that their calls for wealth redistribution were unrealistic and counterproductive. He argued that the wealthy had earned their fortunes through hard work and innovation and that they shouldn't be punished for their success. He also contended that capitalism, despite its flaws, was still the best economic system ever devised and that any attempt to tamper with it would lead to disastrous consequences.

The exchange between O'Leary and Hedges became increasingly contentious, with both men refusing to back down from their positions. In the end, Hedges said he would never appear on the show again, comparing the CBC to the conservative-leaning Fox News.

O'Leary's behavior on the show drew criticism from viewers and media commentators. Many felt that he had crossed a line with his disrespectful remarks toward Hedges and his dismissive attitude toward the Occupy Wall

Street movement. Some demanded his removal from the show.

The CBC's ombudsman, an independent official tasked with upholding the broadcaster's journalistic standards, launched an investigation into the matter. After reviewing the segment in question, the ombudsman concluded that O'Leary's behavior had violated the CBC's journalistic standards. The ombudsman found that O'Leary's remarks were "dismissive and disrespectful" and that they had created a "hostile and intimidating environment" for Hedges. Despite the ombudsman's findings, O'Leary remained unapologetic. He defended his right to express his opinions, even if they were unpopular or controversial. He also reiterated his belief that the Occupy Wall Street movement was misguided and that its calls for wealth redistribution were misguided.

This incident was not the only time that O'Leary's views on wealth and inequality sparked controversy. In January 2014, during another episode of "The Lang and O'Leary Exchange," he made headlines with his comments on the growing gap between the rich and the poor. During the segment, O'Leary was discussing a recent report that showed the world's wealthiest 85 individuals possessed as much wealth as the poorest 3.5 billion people combined. Instead of expressing concern about this staggering statistic, O'Leary celebrated it.

"It's fantastic," he declared. "This is a great thing because it inspires everybody, gets them motivated to look up to the 1% and say, 'I want to become one of those people, I'm going to fight hard to get up to the top.' This is fantastic news, and, of course, I applaud it. What can be wrong with this? I celebrate capitalism."

O'Leary's comments drew immediate condemnation from those who saw them as insensitive and out of touch. Critics argued that his celebration of wealth inequality was not only morally repugnant but also economically unsustainable. They pointed to the fact that extreme inequality can lead to social unrest, political instability, and economic stagnation. O'Leary remained unfazed by the criticism, maintaining that his views were simply a reflection of reality. He argued that wealth inequality was an inevitable consequence of capitalism and that any attempt to artificially level the playing field would only stifle innovation and economic growth.

"Don't tell me that you want to redistribute wealth again," he said. "That's never gonna happen... Redistribution of wealth doesn't work, we tried it in the Soviet Union, North Korea, would you like to live there?"

O'Leary's comments on wealth redistribution reflect his deeply held belief in the power of the free market. He argues that government intervention in the economy is almost always counterproductive and that the best way to create prosperity is to enable individuals and businesses to pursue their own self-interest without interference. This philosophy is rooted in O'Leary's own experiences as an entrepreneur. He has often spoken about the challenges he faced in building his businesses, and he credits his success to his hard work, determination, and willingness to take risks. He believes that anyone, regardless of their background, can achieve success if they are willing to put in the effort.

However, critics argue that O'Leary's focus on individual responsibility ignores the structural inequalities that exist in society. They point to the fact that factors such as race, gender, and socioeconomic status can have a significant impact on a person's opportunities for success.

They argue that government policies aimed at addressing these inequalities are necessary to create a more just and equitable society. His critics argue that his views are out of touch with the realities faced by many ordinary people. They contend that his unwavering belief in the free market and his celebration of wealth inequality ignore the very real problems caused by economic disparity. Whether one agrees with him or not, there is no denying that Kevin O'Leary is a force to be reckoned with. His outspoken nature and controversial views have made him a lightning rod for both praise and criticism, but one thing is certain: he is not afraid to challenge conventional wisdom and spark debate.

Terrence Thomas Kevin O'Leary, a prominent figure in the world of business and television, has carved a multifaceted career that spans entrepreneurship, investing, and media personality. His journey, characterized by sharp wit, financial acumen, and a penchant for the spotlight, has led him to become a recognizable face on both Canadian and American television.

O'Leary's foray into the entertainment industry began with a comedic twist. In 2009, he took the stage at the Winnipeg Comedy Festival, hosting a gala titled "Savings & Groans." The event featured a sketch reminiscent of his role on the popular reality show "Dragon's Den," where aspiring entrepreneurs pitch their business ideas to a panel of investors. In this comedic rendition, O'Leary engaged with comedians Sean Cullen and Ron Sparks, who humorously attempted to secure his investment in their invention – the wheel. This lighthearted performance, which aired on CBC in 2010, showcased O'Leary's ability to embrace humor while maintaining his business-savvy persona.

Following his comedic venture, O'Leary continued to explore his presence in the television realm. In 2012, he co-produced and hosted the reality show "Redemption Inc.," which aired on CBC for one season. The show provided a unique platform for ten ex-convicts, offering them a chance to pitch their business ideas to O'Leary in the hopes of securing funding and a fresh start. This project reflected O'Leary's interest in social entrepreneurship and his belief in providing opportunities for individuals seeking to rebuild their lives.

O'Leary's media presence extended beyond reality television. He also served as a co-host of "SqueezePlay" on Bell Media's Business News Network (BNN), further solidifying his position as a prominent voice in the business world. In 2014, he expanded his reach by joining the Discovery Channel as a contributor for its radio and television stations, including CTV. This move allowed him to share his insights and expertise with a wider audience, cementing his status as a sought-after commentator on business and finance.

In addition to his regular television appearances, O'Leary has made notable guest spots on various programs. In 2015, he participated in the game show "Celebrity Jeopardy," where he showcased his knowledge and competitive spirit. Despite finishing third, he secured a $10,000 donation for his chosen charity. Later that year, O'Leary's discerning eye and charismatic presence landed him a role as a celebrity judge in the 95th Miss America pageant, further demonstrating his versatility and appeal across different entertainment formats.

O'Leary's media ventures extended beyond television, as he explored the world of podcasts in 2018. He hosted the podcast "Ask Mr. Wonderful" for seven episodes, offering listeners a glimpse into his business philosophies and providing advice on a range of financial topics. This platform allowed him to connect with a broader audience and share his insights in a more intimate and conversational format. In 2019, he continued his engagement with online audiences by regularly posting videos on YouTube, once again under the title "Ask Mr. Wonderful." These videos further solidified his online presence and provided a platform for him to share his expertise with a global audience.

O'Leary's most recent television endeavor brought him back to the realm of financial disputes and decision-making. In 2021, he joined CNBC's "Money Court," where he, along with Katie Phang and Ada Pozo, served as an adjudicator in financial disagreements. This role allowed him to leverage his extensive business experience and provide guidance to individuals and businesses seeking resolution to their financial conflicts.

Beyond his media endeavors, O'Leary maintains a prominent role in the business world. He currently serves as a member of ARHT Media's Board of Advisors, alongside renowned Canadian singer Paul Anka and Mexican telecommunications magnate Carlos Slim. This position reflects his continued influence and involvement in innovative companies and his commitment to fostering growth and development in the business sector.

Terrence Thomas Kevin O'Leary's career trajectory showcases a unique blend of business acumen, media savvy, and a captivating personality. From his early entrepreneurial ventures to his prominent roles on television and in the business world, O'Leary has consistently demonstrated his ability to adapt, innovate, and captivate audiences. His journey serves as an inspiration to aspiring entrepreneurs and a testament to the power of combining business expertise with a strong media presence. As he continues to explore new avenues and contribute to the business and entertainment landscape, O'Leary's impact is sure to be felt for years to come.

Chapter Four

All About His Political Activities

Kevin O'Leary stands out as a figure of both admiration and controversy. His journey from the world of reality television to the political arena has been marked by bold pronouncements, unwavering determination, and a commitment to fiscal responsibility that has resonated with many Canadians. O'Leary's interest in Canadian politics became increasingly apparent in the mid-2010s. In January 2016, he made a highly publicized offer to invest $1 million in the economy of Alberta, but with a significant caveat: the resignation of then-Premier Rachel Notley. This bold move, though ultimately unsuccessful, signaled O'Leary's growing dissatisfaction with the political status quo and his willingness to leverage his personal wealth to influence change.

His engagement with the political landscape deepened in February 2016 when he appeared at a conference for federal Conservatives alongside four prospective leadership candidates. During his presentation, titled "If I Run, This is How," O'Leary outlined his vision for the country and boldly predicted the downfall of the Liberal government within four years due to economic collapse. This confident assertion, while not coming to fruition, underscored his belief in his own political acumen and his conviction that he could steer the country in a more prosperous direction.

The resignation of Stephen Harper as leader of the Conservative Party of Canada in 2016 created a void in the party's leadership, and O'Leary's attendance at Conservative Party gatherings in February and May of that year fueled speculation about his potential candidacy in the upcoming 2017 leadership election. His presence at these events, coupled with his outspoken views on economic and political matters, positioned him as a potential frontrunner in the race. However, O'Leary's foray into the political arena was not without its challenges. In February 2016, Maxime Bernier, a prominent Conservative Quebecois politician, launched a critique of O'Leary's candidacy, labeling him a "tourist" due to his inability to speak French. Bernier emphasized the importance of French language proficiency for any aspiring prime minister, implicitly questioning O'Leary's commitment to representing all Canadians.

In response to this criticism, O'Leary acknowledged the significance of French language skills and pledged to learn French in preparation for the next federal election. He maintained that his focus on economic issues transcended linguistic barriers and that his vision for the country would resonate with Canadians of all backgrounds.

On January 18, 2017, O'Leary officially declared his candidacy for the Conservative leadership, formalizing his ambition to lead the party and the country. This announcement was met with mixed reactions. Some praised his business acumen and outsider perspective, while others expressed concerns about his lack of political experience and his sometimes abrasive personality. Among those who expressed reservations about O'Leary's candidacy was his former Dragons' Den co-star Arlene Dickinson. She characterized O'Leary as being too "self-interested and opportunistic" to hold the office of prime minister, suggesting that his motivations were rooted more in personal ambition than in genuine public service. In contrast, another former Dragons' Den co-star, W. Brett Wilson, came out in support of O'Leary's candidacy. Wilson highlighted the distinction between O'Leary's public persona as a shrewd businessman and his underlying character, suggesting that his television portrayal did not fully capture his capabilities and intentions.

O'Leary's candidacy injected a new dynamic into the Conservative leadership race, drawing attention from both supporters and detractors. His background as a successful entrepreneur and television personality set him apart from traditional politicians, and his focus on economic growth and fiscal responsibility resonated with a segment of the electorate. Throughout his campaign, O'Leary emphasized his belief in the power of free markets, limited government intervention, and individual responsibility. He advocated for lower taxes, reduced regulation, and a balanced budget, arguing that these measures would stimulate economic growth and create jobs. O'Leary's campaign also highlighted his outsider status, portraying him as a non-politician who could bring a fresh perspective to Ottawa. He positioned himself as a pragmatic problem-solver, not beholden to special interests or ideological dogma.

In the final stages of the leadership race, O'Leary emerged as a frontrunner, alongside Maxime Bernier and Andrew Scheer. The contest became a three-way race, with each candidate vying for the support of party members. O'Leary's campaign focused on his economic vision, his outsider status, and his ability to defeat the Liberal government in the next federal election. He presented himself as the candidate of change, promising to shake up Ottawa and put the country on a path to prosperity.

In the final ballot, O'Leary finished third, behind Andrew Scheer and Maxime Bernier. While he did not win the leadership, his campaign had a significant impact on the Conservative Party and the Canadian political landscape. O'Leary's candidacy brought new attention to economic issues and the need for fiscal responsibility. His outsider status and his focus on change resonated with many Canadians, and his campaign helped to energize the Conservative Party base. Although O'Leary's political aspirations did not ultimately come to fruition, his foray into the political arena left a lasting mark. His willingness to challenge the status quo, his focus on economic growth, and his appeal to a segment of the electorate demonstrated his potential as a political force. While his future in politics remains uncertain, Kevin O'Leary's journey from reality television to the political stage serves as a testament to his ambition, his determination, and his unwavering belief in his own abilities. Whether he returns to the political arena or continues to pursue his business ventures, O'Leary's impact on Canadian society is undeniable.

Kevin O'Leary has had a career marked by both success and controversy. One such incident occurred on February 1, 2017, when O'Leary posted a video of himself shooting at a Miami gun range. The timing of the post coincided with the funeral for three victims of the Quebec City mosque shooting, which had taken place just days earlier. This sparked immediate backlash, with many criticizing O'Leary for his insensitivity. The video was quickly removed from Facebook out of respect for the victims and their families. It was also revealed that O'Leary was in New York promoting one of his business ventures at the time of the post, further fueling the criticism. O'Leary later apologized for the timing of the post, saying he had not been aware of the funeral when he shared the video.

This incident occurred during O'Leary's campaign for the leadership of the Conservative Party of Canada. Despite being a frontrunner in the polls, O'Leary dropped out of the race on April 26, 2017. He cited a lack of support in Quebec as a major factor in his decision, stating that it would be difficult to defeat Justin Trudeau in the 2019 federal election without strong support in the province. O'Leary endorsed Maxime Bernier, another frontrunner for the position, upon dropping out. Andrew Scheer, who narrowly edged out Bernier eventually won the leadership election. This incident provides a glimpse into the complex and often controversial nature of Kevin O'Leary's public persona. While he is known for his business acumen and sharp wit, he has also been criticized for his insensitivity and lack of political awareness. The gun range video incident serves as a reminder that even the most successful individuals can make mistakes, and that the timing and context of one's actions can have significant consequences.

Terrence Thomas Kevin O'Leary is a prominent figure in the world of business and finance, has established himself as a fervent advocate for free market principles and fiscal conservatism. His outspoken views on economic policy, particularly his staunch support for unfettered trade and his vehement opposition to excessive taxation and government intervention, have placed him at the forefront of many economic debates.

O'Leary's unwavering belief in the power of free trade is perhaps most evident in his vocal support for multilateral agreements such as the North American Free Trade Agreement (NAFTA). He views such agreements as vital tools for promoting economic growth and prosperity, arguing that they facilitate the seamless flow of goods and services across borders, thereby enhancing efficiency and productivity. His stance on this issue has led him to criticize protectionist measures, which he believes hinder economic progress and harm consumers by limiting choice and driving up prices.

In line with his free market perspective, O'Leary maintains that corporate tax rates in Canada are excessively high, creating a significant drag on business investment and job creation. He contends that lower taxes would incentivize companies to expand their operations, leading to increased economic activity and higher wages for workers. O'Leary's commitment to this principle is so strong that he has pledged to eliminate the national carbon tax, a levy on fossil fuels designed to curb greenhouse gas emissions. He argues that this tax disproportionately burdens businesses and consumers, ultimately stifling economic growth.

Furthermore, O'Leary has adopted a confrontational approach to advancing his tax-cutting agenda, even threatening to withhold transfer payments from provinces that refuse to abolish their own carbon taxes. This tactic underscores his determination to reduce the overall tax burden on Canadians, which he sees as a crucial step towards fostering a more dynamic and competitive economy.

O'Leary's fiscal conservatism extends beyond tax policy to encompass a deep-seated aversion to deficit spending. He is a vocal critic of governments that accumulate debt, arguing that such practices are unsustainable and jeopardize the long-term health of the economy. He advocates for a balanced budget approach, emphasizing the importance of living within one's means and avoiding the accumulation of excessive debt. O'Leary believes that eliminating the national debt should be a top priority for any government, as it would free up resources for investment in critical areas such as education, infrastructure, and healthcare.

Beyond his views on taxation and government spending, O'Leary has also expressed strong opinions on a range of other economic issues. He is a vocal opponent of government control over Canada's telecommunications system, arguing that the Canadian Radio-television and Telecommunications Commission (CRTC) stifles innovation and competition in the industry. He believes that a more deregulated approach would lead to lower prices, better service, and greater choice for consumers.

O'Leary's outspokenness has not been confined to Canadian economic policies. He has also weighed in on American political figures, criticizing Rep. Alexandria Ocasio-Cortez for her support of higher corporate taxes. He contends that such policies would have a devastating impact on the economy, leading to job losses and reduced investment.

On the issue of labor rights, O'Leary has taken a stance that some may consider controversial. He opposes "right to disconnect" legislation, which would give employees the legal right to ignore work-related communications outside of working hours. He argues that such legislation would be detrimental to productivity and harm businesses' ability to compete in a globalized economy.

In the realm of energy policy, O'Leary has emerged as a strong proponent of energy independence for Canada. He supports the construction of a pipeline from the Athabasca oil sands to Eastern Canada, arguing that this would reduce Canada's reliance on foreign oil and create jobs in the energy sector. He has also expressed support for a national referendum on the issue of pipelines, demonstrating his commitment to democratic decision-making on critical energy infrastructure projects. Throughout his career, Kevin O'Leary has consistently championed free market principles and fiscal responsibility. His views, often delivered with his characteristic bluntness, have sparked debate and challenged conventional thinking on a wide range of economic issues. Whether one agrees with him or not, there is no denying that O'Leary has made a significant impact on the economic discourse in Canada and beyond. His unwavering commitment to his beliefs, combined with his business acumen and media savvy, have cemented his status as a prominent voice in the ongoing debate about the role of government in the economy.

Unlike the hard-nosed image he often projects in business, O'Leary identifies his social policies as "very liberal." He is a vocal supporter of same-sex marriage, believing that individuals should have the freedom to marry whomever they choose, regardless of gender. Similarly, he advocates for transgender rights, recognizing the importance of respecting individuals' gender identities and expressions. O'Leary's stance on marijuana reflects a pragmatic approach. He supports legalizing and regulating the substance, viewing it as a potential source of tax revenue and a way to reduce the burden on the legal system associated with marijuana-related offenses. His position aligns with a growing trend toward accepting and legalizing marijuana in various parts of the world.

On the sensitive issue of assisted suicide, O'Leary takes a clear position. He supports the practice, viewing it as a matter of personal choice and individual autonomy. He points to Switzerland as a successful model for assisted suicide, where it has been legal and regulated for many years. In matters of foreign and military policy, O'Leary demonstrates a thoughtful and sometimes unconventional approach. He opposed Canadian airstrikes on ISIS, arguing for a more restrained military

105

role in the Syrian Civil War. He envisioned Canada taking on a peacekeeping role instead, contributing to the stability of the region without engaging in direct combat.

O'Leary's perspective on Russia is nuanced. In a 2017 interview, he described Russia as "neither an ally nor a foe," recognizing the complexities of the relationship between the two countries. He avoids simplistic categorizations and prefers to assess the situation based on its specific circumstances. Regarding military procurement, O'Leary has been critical of Justin Trudeau's plan. He advocates the purchase of aerial combat drones to defend Canadian airspace, arguing that they offer a cost-effective solution for national defense. He also supports phasing out the use of the Lockheed CP-140 Aurora, citing its high cost and the potential for more efficient alternatives.

O'Leary is a strong proponent of a well-funded military. He has criticized the perceived lack of funding for the Canadian Armed Forces and supports increasing military expenditures to the NATO-recommended 2% of GDP. He believes a strong military is essential for national security and Canada's ability to defend its interests on the global stage. On immigration, O'Leary proposes a practical approach to attract and retain skilled immigrants. He suggests creating a "fast track" for citizenship for those who graduate from Canadian colleges or universities and secure employment. This expedited process would also extend to their spouses and children, providing a more efficient pathway for families to establish themselves in Canada. While welcoming skilled immigrants, O'Leary also emphasizes the importance of border security. He advocates increased measures to address irregular border crossings, ensuring that immigration processes are followed and that the integrity of the system is maintained. O'Leary's views on the Senate are unconventional and thought-provoking. He proposes that Senators should pay money every year instead of receiving a salary. This, he argues, would transform the Senate from a "cost centre to Canada" into a "profit centre." His proposal challenges the traditional Senate concept and raises questions about its role and function in Canadian politics.

In the autumn of 2018, a legal dispute emerged that would pit Kevin O'Leary against the very institutions governing the Canadian electoral process. O'Leary, known for his business acumen and sharp investments, found himself embroiled in a controversy surrounding campaign finance regulations. At the heart of the matter was a law that limited candidates' use of personal funds for their leadership campaigns to a mere $25,000. This restriction became a point of contention for O'Leary, who had incurred a significant debt during his unsuccessful bid for the leadership of the Conservative Party of Canada. O'Leary's financial obligation amounted to $430,000, a substantial sum that he proposed to settle immediately using his own resources. His plan involved reimbursing himself later through fundraising efforts. However, Elections Canada, the independent body responsible for administering federal elections, rejected this proposal, deeming it a violation of campaign finance regulations. The agency maintained that such a maneuver would circumvent the spending limits imposed on candidates, thereby undermining the principles of fair and transparent elections.

O'Leary's response was swift and resolute. He engaged the services of prominent lawyer Joseph Groia, renowned for his expertise in securities law and complex litigation. Together, they initiated legal proceedings against Elections Canada and the federal elections commissioner, challenging the constitutionality of the campaign finance laws. O'Leary's legal challenge centered on the argument that restrictions on using personal funds violate his fundamental rights as a Canadian citizen. Specifically, O'Leary contended that the $25,000 limit on personal spending violated his Section 2 Charter right to free expression. This right, enshrined in the Canadian Charter of Rights and Freedoms, guarantees individuals the freedom to express their thoughts, beliefs, and opinions without undue government interference. O'Leary argued that the financial constraints imposed by the law effectively silenced wealthy individuals who wished to participate in the political arena. He believed that this restriction created an uneven playing field, favoring those with access to extensive donor networks while hindering those who wished to self-fund their campaigns. O'Leary asserted that the threat of imprisonment for exceeding the spending limit violated his Section 7 Charter right to security of the person. This right protects individuals from arbitrary detention or imprisonment and ensures that any deprivation of liberty is in accordance with the principles of fundamental justice. O'Leary argued that the severity of the penalty for exceeding the spending limit was disproportionate and constituted an unreasonable infringement on his personal liberty.

O'Leary's legal challenge sparked a public debate about the role of money in politics and the balance between free expression and the need to regulate campaign financing. Supporters of the existing laws argued that they were necessary to prevent wealthy individuals from unduly influencing elections and to ensure that all candidates had a fair chance to compete. They maintained that the limits on personal spending promoted a more level playing field and prevented the perception that the highest bidder could buy elections. Critics of the laws, on the other hand, argued that they unfairly restricted individuals' ability to participate in the democratic process. They contended that the limits on personal spending favored career politicians and those with established fundraising networks, while hindering newcomers and those who wished to self-fund their campaigns. They also argued that the laws infringed on the freedom of expression, as they limited the ability of individuals to use their own resources to promote their political views. O'Leary's legal challenge brought these competing perspectives into sharp focus, highlighting the complex and often contentious nature of campaign finance regulations. The case raised fundamental questions about the balance between individual rights and the need to maintain the integrity of the electoral process.

Chapter Five

Books And Bibliography

In September 2011, Kevin O'Leary entered the literary world with his debut book, "Cold Hard Truth: On Business, Money & Life." Within its pages, he offered readers a glimpse into his perspectives on a range of topics, from the complexities of family relationships and the dynamics of investing to the broader subjects of money and life itself. This initial foray into writing marked the beginning of O'Leary's exploration of sharing his insights and experiences with a wider audience.

Following the success of his first book, O'Leary continued his writing journey with a sequel published in 2012, titled "The Cold Hard Truth on Men, Women, and Money: 50 Common Money Mistakes and How to Fix Them." This book focused on the critical importance of cultivating financial literacy and financial education as the cornerstones of building and achieving financial abundance, freedom, and stability. O'Leary emphasized the need for individuals to take control of their financial destinies by equipping themselves with the knowledge and skills necessary to make informed decisions about their money.

In 2015, O'Leary further expanded his literary contributions with another book that examined a variety of important life choices. He explored topics ranging from education and career paths to managing personal finances, romantic relationships, marriage, raising children, family bonds, and retirement planning. Recognizing the interconnectedness of these aspects of life, O'Leary provided readers with guidance on navigating these choices effectively.

Within this book, O'Leary also addressed the challenges associated with parenting and nurturing a family while simultaneously striving to provide financial security and wealth for them. He acknowledged the delicate balance between fulfilling familial responsibilities and pursuing financial success, offering insights into how to manage both effectively.

Furthermore, O'Leary offered guidance on managing one's personal financial situation, emphasizing the importance of instilling financial literacy values within family members. He encouraged the development of habits such as saving and investing money, and the proper and proficient management of loans, debts, and credit. By sharing his knowledge and experiences, O'Leary sought to empower readers to make sound financial decisions and build a secure financial future.

O'Leary's books reflect his belief in the power of financial education and responsible financial management. He advocates for individuals to take control of their financial lives, make informed choices, and build a solid foundation for themselves and their families. Through his writing, he shares his insights and experiences, aiming to provide readers with the tools and knowledge necessary to achieve financial success and stability.

Chapter Six

Personal life Family And Relationships

Terrence Thomas Kevin O'Leary, widely recognized by his middle name, Kevin, is a man of deep-seated faith, identifying as a devout Catholic. This spiritual foundation has likely played a significant role in shaping his worldview and values, influencing his personal and professional life. In 1990, he exchanged vows with Linda Greer, beginning a journey of marriage that has spanned decades. Their relationship, however, has not been without its challenges. In 2011, the couple faced a period of separation, a decision that undoubtedly tested their commitment. Yet, their bond proved resilient, and after a two-year hiatus, they reconciled, reaffirming their love and dedication to each other.

Their union has been blessed with two children, Trevor and Savannah, who have grown up witnessing their parents' entrepreneurship and dedication. O'Leary, reflecting on the delicate balance between professional pursuits and family life, once acknowledged the consuming nature of a thriving business. He recognized the sacrifices required to achieve success, emphasizing that the rewards of such dedication often come later in life, allowing individuals to provide for their families in ways others may not be able to. This perspective underscores his belief that the freedom and financial security attained through hard work are valuable outcomes of a successful career. The O'Learys have established a life that embraces multiple locations, reflecting their cosmopolitan lifestyle and diverse interests. Their primary residences are in the vibrant city of Miami Beach, Florida, and the bustling metropolis of Toronto, Canada. These contrasting environments offer a stimulating blend of urban energy and cultural richness. In addition to their city dwellings, the O'Learys find solace and tranquility in a cottage nestled in Muskoka, Ontario. This picturesque region, known for its stunning natural beauty and serene lakes, provides a welcome escape from the demands of their busy lives. The cottage serves as a place for relaxation, recreation, and quality time with family and friends. Further expanding their global footprint, the O'Learys maintain residences in Boston, Massachusetts, and Geneva, Switzerland. These locations reflect their international connections and appreciation for diverse cultures. Boston, a hub of academic excellence and historical significance, offers a stimulating environment for intellectual pursuits. Geneva, renowned for its financial institutions and cosmopolitan atmosphere, provides a gateway to European business and cultural experiences.

In a 2022 CNBC interview, O'Leary revealed an intriguing addition to his international portfolio: UAE citizenship. This strategic move grants him access to a dynamic business landscape and facilitates partnerships with Emirati investors. It exemplifies his proactive approach to expanding his investment opportunities and global network. One of his enduring passions is professional sports. O'Leary is an ardent supporter of the New England Patriots, a team renowned for its winning tradition and strategic gameplay. His dedication to the Patriots goes beyond casual observation; he is a dedicated fan who makes a point of watching every game, regardless of his location or the hour. Whether he finds himself in the familiar surroundings of his home or traversing the globe on business ventures, O'Leary ensures that he remains connected to his team, following their triumphs and setbacks with unwavering loyalty. This commitment to the Patriots speaks to a sense of constancy and an appreciation for the pursuit of excellence, qualities that resonate with O'Leary's own approach to business. Beyond the gridiron, O'Leary finds solace and satisfaction in the world of fine wine. He is a connoisseur, a member of the Confrérie des Chevaliers du Tastevin, an exclusive international association dedicated to the appreciation of Burgundy wines. This organization, steeped in tradition and renowned for its discerning membership, counts O'Leary among its ranks, a testament to his refined palate and his passion for the intricacies of winemaking. His involvement in this esteemed society provides a glimpse into a side of O'Leary that contrasts with his public persona. It reveals an appreciation for the finer things in life, a recognition of the artistry and dedication required to produce a truly exceptional vintage.

O'Leary's interests extend beyond the realm of spectator sports and the pleasures of the table. He is also a dedicated photographer, a pursuit he has cultivated throughout his life. His passion for photography has led him to exhibit and sell his work, transforming his artistic endeavors into philanthropic acts. The proceeds from the sale of his photographs are donated to charitable causes, reflecting O'Leary's commitment to giving back to the community and using his talents to support those in need. This dedication to philanthropy adds another dimension to his character, showcasing a sense of social responsibility that runs parallel to his entrepreneurial spirit. Besides his other passions, O'Leary is an avid collector and watch connoisseur. This fascination with horology reflects his appreciation for craftsmanship, precision, and the intricate mechanics that drive these miniature marvels of engineering. O'Leary often shares his knowledge and enthusiasm for watches on social media platforms and even on Shark Tank, offering insights into the history, design, and value of various timepieces. This passion provides another avenue for O'Leary to connect with his audience, showcasing a personal interest that extends beyond the realm of business and finance. These diverse interests paint a fuller picture of Kevin O'Leary, revealing a man of multifaceted passions and hidden depths. While he may be best known for his business acumen and his no-nonsense approach to investing, O'Leary's personal pursuits provide a glimpse into the man behind the public persona. They showcase a dedication to excellence, a refined taste, and a commitment to philanthropy, all of which contribute to a more nuanced understanding of this complex and captivating figure.

Chapter Seven

O'Leary Boating Accident

In the summer of 2019, a tragic event unfolded on the serene waters of Lake Joseph in Muskoka, Ontario, casting a shadow over the life of renowned businessman and television personality, Kevin O'Leary. On the evening of August 24th, O'Leary and his wife, Linda, were aboard their boat when a devastating collision occurred with another vessel. The incident resulted in the loss of two lives, a 64-year-old man and a 48-year-old woman, who were occupants of the other boat. The immediate aftermath of the crash was marked by shock and confusion. O'Leary, in a public statement, expressed his deep sorrow for the victims and their families, emphasizing his full cooperation with the ongoing police investigation. He maintained that the other boat involved in the collision was operating without its navigation lights, a crucial safety measure, and further claimed that it left the scene before authorities arrived. However, the police report later clarified that both boats had left the scene to reach a location where they could contact emergency services.

As the investigation progressed, the focus shifted towards determining culpability and potential charges. On September 24th, 2019, Linda O'Leary was formally charged with careless operation of a vessel under the small vessel regulations of the Canada Shipping Act. This charge carried the potential for a maximum sentence of 18 months imprisonment and a $10,000 fine. Richard Ruh, the operator of the other boat, also faced charges for failing to exhibit navigation lights while underway. The legal proceedings surrounding the incident garnered significant media attention, with the public closely following the developments. On October 11th, 2019, the Public Prosecution Service of

Canada announced that Linda O'Leary would not face jail time if convicted. The trial commenced, and after a period of legal proceedings, Linda O'Leary was found not guilty of careless operation of the vessel on September 14th, 2021.

The Lake Joseph boat crash was a poignant reminder of the fragility of life and the profound consequences that can arise from unforeseen events. It thrust Kevin O'Leary and his family into the center of a legal battle, testing their resilience and challenging their public image. While the legal proceedings have concluded, the emotional scars of the incident may linger, shaping their perspectives and actions in the years to come.

Conclusion: The Legacy of Mr. Wonderful

Terrence Thomas Kevin O'Leary, the man known as "Mr. Wonderful," is a multifaceted individual whose impact spans the realms of business, investing, politics, and entertainment. His journey, as we've explored throughout this biography, is a testament to the power of ambition, resilience, and a relentless pursuit of success. From his early entrepreneurial endeavors to his prominent role on Shark Tank, O'Leary has consistently defied expectations and carved his own path.

O'Leary's story is one of contradictions. He is a shrewd businessman with a sharp tongue, yet he possesses a charismatic charm that resonates with audiences. He is a ruthless negotiator who demands accountability, yet he also demonstrates a willingness to mentor and support those he believes in. This complex personality has made him both a polarizing figure and a source of inspiration for aspiring entrepreneurs.

One of the defining characteristics of O'Leary's career is his ability to adapt and reinvent himself. He transitioned from the software industry to the world of television with remarkable ease, leveraging his business acumen and outspoken personality to become a household name. His willingness to embrace new challenges and explore different avenues has undoubtedly contributed to his longevity and success.

O'Leary's impact on the business world is undeniable. As an investor, he has helped countless entrepreneurs realize their dreams, providing them with the capital and guidance needed to grow their businesses. His involvement in Shark Tank has not only brought him fame and fortune but has also democratized access to funding for small businesses, inspiring a new generation of innovators.

Beyond his business ventures, O'Leary has also made his mark in the political arena. His foray into politics, though ultimately unsuccessful, highlighted his desire to contribute to his country and shape public policy. While his views may not always align with the mainstream, his willingness to engage in the political discourse speaks to his commitment to making a difference.

O'Leary's legacy extends beyond his financial success and television appearances. He has become a cultural icon, known for his candid advice, his no-nonsense attitude, and his unwavering belief in the power of capitalism. His catchphrases, such as "You're dead to me," have become part of the popular lexicon, and his image as a tough but fair investor has resonated with audiences worldwide. However, O'Leary's legacy is not without its critics. Some have accused him of being overly harsh and insensitive in his dealings with entrepreneurs. Others have questioned his business practices and his political views. Despite these criticisms, O'Leary remains a force to be reckoned with, a testament to the power of self-belief and determination.

In assessing O'Leary's impact, it is important to acknowledge his contributions to entrepreneurship and his role in popularizing business education. Through his investments, his television appearances, and his books, he has demystified the world of business and inspired countless individuals to pursue their entrepreneurial dreams. His emphasis on financial literacy and his practical advice have empowered people from all walks of life to take control of their financial futures.

As we conclude this biography, it is clear that Kevin O'Leary is a complex and fascinating figure who has left an indelible mark on the world. He is a businessman, investor, politician and entertainer. He is a man who has defied expectations, embraced challenges, and achieved remarkable success. Whether you admire him or criticize him, there is no denying that Kevin O'Leary is a force to be reckoned with, a true original who has earned his place in the pantheon of Canadian business icons.

His story serves as a reminder that success is not always linear, that setbacks are inevitable, and that perseverance is key. O'Leary's journey is a testament to the power of ambition, the importance of adaptability, and the value of staying true to oneself. As he continues to evolve and explore new ventures, one thing is certain: Kevin O'Leary will continue to captivate audiences and leave his mark on the world for years to come.